KATRINA, OUR STORY

Journal of Mary S. Landry

Bloomington, IN

authorHOUSE®

Milton Keynes, UK

AuthorHouse™
1663 Liberty Drive, Suite 200
Bloomington, IN 47403
www.authorhouse.com
Phone: 1-800-839-8640

AuthorHouse™ UK Ltd.
500 Avebury Boulevard
Central Milton Keynes, MK9 2BE
www.authorhouse.co.uk
Phone: 08001974150

First published by AuthorHouse 8/21/2006

ISBN: 1-4259-4585-6 (e)
ISBN: 1-4259-4584-8 (sc)

Library of Congress Control Number: 2006905465

Printed in the United States of America
Bloomington, Indiana

This book is printed on acid-free paper.

Acknowledgments

I thank Our Lord for his bounty and grace, which I know I do not deserve but am ever grateful.

Special thanks goes to my ever-loving and greatest supporter, and friend, my husband, Michael Landry .

I would like to thank the rest of my family, both immediate and extended, and friends for the inspiration and encouragement to pursue my writing career. Sometimes we don't recognize the beauty, skills or talents with which we are blessed by God until others eek it out of us.

I hope I haven't left any out, but here are a few specific names that I wish to recognize as having urged me on in my struggle to discover a career path.

Carol Largent
Mary Anita Reynaud
Sandy Tackett

KATRINA – Day of Destruction

Day [-1] (Saturday 8/27/05)

We found out today through the news that the unfortunate people of Florida had endured yet another storm. Sure Katrina was only a Category 1 storm, but she left her mark on Miami with flooding, building damage and lost lives numbering less than 10 Still, there were nearly one million out of electrical power for several days. It seems that Florida's fate was to be the continual target of Mother Nature's wrath

We watched the news and the weathermen expect Katrina to strengthen when she enters the Gulf from the Atlantic. It seems that we may get some of the outer bands and the accompanying rough weather I decided to attend vigil mass today at St. Peter's Catholic Church because I won't be able to attend the Traditional mass at St. Patrick's in New Orleans because the city officials have ordered evacuations in many parts, if not all, of the metropolitan areas that are subject to flooding. The newest plan for evacuation includes a contra-flow program that systematically closes major thoroughfares to two-way traffic and alleviates traffic backups caused by the mass exodus of evacuees. I don't know the city's actual emergency plan, but it seems that complete abandonment of the city is not the complete answer to saving lives and bouncing back after anticipated destruction. But because this plan for evacuation would be effective tomorrow, I did not want to attempt to deal with the traffic situation. At mass, I saw my mother and father there also. My son,

Mathew G. accompanied me, as well. In my prayers, I asked Our Lady of Prompt Succor to pray for our community and families, just in case the storm would venture our way.

Mike worked on his side jobs today and I cooked dinner. The forecasts this evening projects the path of Katrina to be between the Louisiana coastline and the Florida panhandle. I fully expect that she will make her way east of New Orleans, like so many times before. My daughter, Megan, is moving home this weekend. She is trying to formulate a new plan for school, work and her life goals. Mathew G. will be leaving for basic training in the Air National Guard in about a month. He is working out and running every day to stay fit for his training. His plan is to be a member of the Guard while attending school at Louisiana Tech in Ruston after his one-year On-The-Job service with the Guard in Air Traffic Control. My step-son, Matthew A., moved in with us in June for us to help him get back on his feet financially and to help him discover a career to pursue. He is working at Waffle House and is due to start a new job at Flowers Bakery (Bunny Bread) in New Orleans on Monday, August 29th. It's a great job with excellent benefits and good pay. Matthew Adam should be back on his feet and ready to be independent again. My mind is working on new plans for the future, duties, chores and other routine activities without a second thought of any danger, but also without any appreciation for the current blessings in my life. It's good to have a house full again.

Day 0 (Sunday 8/28/05)

When I awake, I take a quick look at the television, just to make sure that Katrina heads east as I fully expect, since it had happened most frequently to us here in St. Tammany Parish during my lifetime of 40 years with the two exceptions that are still the most talked about: Betsy and Camille. Betsy hit New Orleans in 1965 as a Category 3 storm causing much flooding. I lived in New Orleans at the time but I was a toddler. My parents did evacuate, even though my father was an extern at Charity Hospital. With three small children at the time, my mother needed more security than the neighbors and city could offer, so Dad worked it out with other doctors on staff who were unmarried, to cover his shifts. Camille came in 1969 as a Category 4 storm but after landfall, becoming a Category 3 storm. I don't have any memory of Camille. Our family lived in Opelousas, further west of New Orleans, at the time. It did not pose much threat there, I guess.

Today, I casually listened to the local weather report while going about my daily routine without much thought or concern. I perked up a bit when I heard the newest prediction. To my utter astonishment, New Orleans and southeastern Louisiana were in the cross-hairs of a raging monster! Katrina had strengthened more than expected and is now a strong Category 4 expected to turn into a Category 5 before making landfall in Southeast Louisiana. I run outside to find my husband, Mike, already strapping down the trees that surround the house. I quickly wake up Mathew G. to go with me to Lowes for lumber and supplies to board up the windows. Matthew Adam is sent to fill up gas cans and everyone is ordered to fill up their vehicle gas tanks. Mike created this tethering system of straps and come-a-longs that he attaches to the trees surrounding the house about 20-40 feet up so that the tree, if it were to fall, would only be able to fall away from the house. He used it once or twice when a storm threatened only to have wasted time doing it because the storm either turned away or was not strong enough to affect the towering pines very much.

Mathew and I enter Lowes. The store is crowded, but not as much as I thought it would be, considering the storm. I actually anticipated that Lowes would be out of plywood. I am thankful that they seem to have plenty, but no employees around to help us load the cart. Finally, we get what we need and wait in line. I watch people scurrying around gathering supplies. We load up the pickup with 10 plywood sheets and 40 2x4's and then grab a bag of washers. Mathew grumbles a bit (like most any teenager) that it's a waste of time and energy. But he's a good son and completes the chore helping his old mom with his muscle. I am amazed at his vigor and strength and very grateful he is with us to help. I explain to him as we drive along that this storm, if staying on its current path, would be different and worse than any we had previously encountered. He listens, but I think a bit skeptically of what this hurricane might bring. The worst situation he has endured was when we lived in our former house on Hoffman Road about 8 miles from our current home. During the Flood of '95, the water there rose to the top step of our porch, about 2 feet. Upon our return home, the trees are secured around the house and Mike has prepared the generators for any short loss of electricity. I don't expect us to have to use it very long, if at all. But I'm glad we have it, just in case.

Mike and the two Mathews begin boarding up the windows and supporting them with braces. The house seems dark. Megan finally arrives to hunker down with us. I was getting worried that she wouldn't make it. It is customary for many families and/or friends to gather under one roof if threatened, usually the family with the space, safer location, and/or emergency supplies or preparations. Many calls were being made to family members. I invited my brother David, Rachel and their kids to come over because their house lies South of the I-12. There is a mandatory evacuation of that area. Rachel defers saying she may go to our parents' home, which is about 2 miles from my home in the rural area north of Abita Springs. David is a firefighter as is my other brother Chris. They will most definitely be working the storm emergencies so it is good peace of mind for them to have other family to rely upon for their wives and children. The last word I hear is that Robert and Ann (another brother & his wife) are staying at their home in old Covington. My brother, Ellis, and his wife, Shannon, are also going to my parent's home. I don't know anything about my brother Paul, or my sister Lori. Mike's parents, Edgar and Geri, actually evacuated! I am relieved but surprised because they have never left their home in Lakeview area of New Orleans. Each storm, we invite them to come, but to no avail. They left with the neighbors to Shreveport. Mike's stepbrother, Darryl, stays to hold down the fort in his house in New Orleans in the Lakeview area. Our son, Billy, and his wife, Sunnie, leave for Lake Charles (in Western Louisiana). She has family there. I'm glad they took the baby away from this area but I'm not sure that the storm won't go their way. I was hoping they would go either north or to Houston, far enough west to be safer. Of our other children, Michael Jr. and his family are safely in New Jersey, and Brian is in the Air Force in Arkansas.

My phone rings and it's our friends the Scariano's. They say they are coming to our home to sleep over and bring a bottle of champagne to have a hurricane party! We laugh about this when I tell Mike they are coming. It's now about 8:00 PM when they arrive. We pour the champagne and laugh and talk. The TV is blaring in the midst of our crowd, now 9 people, with the local news showing the powerful storm now aiming directly at us.

Katrina's winds are now 175 miles per hour and she is a Cat 5. Her eye is perfectly rounded and the storm is swirling around that center in a beautiful and yet deadly symmetry. I am amazed at the breadth of her, over 300 miles wide. I am feeling nervous about her gathering herself together, at once organized and chaotic. I have watched hundreds of other storms on the radar and satellite broadcasts, but she had me spellbound like a rabbit in the beam of a flashlight

Steve and Dianne Scariano are good friends. Steve is a professor at Loyola University in New Orleans where his son, Johnny, is a sophomore this fall. They have a younger son, David, in high school. Steve is charismatic and entertaining. Dianne, a housewife, mother and artist, helps me to put away the food I have prepared and then we set up the sleeping arrangements. They brought the air mattresses for the floors and some snacks, movies and Sammy, the rat terrier. Jinx, my cat isn't too happy, but this should be fun! We think we can expect a few limbs to clean up and some rain, and we know we won't have to work tomorrow! That feeling was a good feeling. The last one I had for a while.

Katrina Day - (Monday 8/29/05)

I am awakened by the sound of the electricity dying. The sound you hear when all of your electrical luxuries click, tick, or beep as they turn off. It's almost like we are so used to the background hums that when silence appears, it's deafening! I quickly come to the living room and we gather to hear the latest. While we slept, Katrina crept up on us The powerful beauty did not slumber, but instead traveled through the night like a locomotive on a set destination, Louisiana. She made landfall in Buras, in lower Plaquemines parish, a small community near the Gulf of Mexico. I am happy that most of Plaquemines parish has evacuated. Grand Isle, a cluster of fishing camps and fishermen, has evacuated all but 5 people. As an island, the residents are used to this process and most avoid staying through hurricanes as they pound the coast in their full fury from the warm Gulf waters.

It's 6:30 AM. Mike starts the generator so that we can see the latest news. Having satellite television is a great luxury. In my childhood, the best we could hope for during hurricanes was a battery-operated radio with a strong capacity for reception. Back then, the coordinates would be given out and every family had a tracking map to mark the location of the storm with a thumbtack or pin. Even in my teens, the television only lasted as long as the power, which was not long. Now we could see on the radar and learn about the wind speeds, location and projected path. What we see on the TV is met with mixed emotions. Bad news - she is heading straight for our area. Good news - she had diminished a bit when she hit the coastal waters to a STRONG Category 4 storm. Also, she is moving faster - around 15 mph. We all know that a fast storm is better. That means it moves through quickly with less time for rain accumulation. Steve is jubilant! "The winds are down, Mike, look at dat the winds are down!" he cries in his heavy New Orleans accent. We all voice our thoughts and projections, but we all know that it is larger and more powerful than anything we have experienced in our lives. My heart pounds rapidly, as the sky darkens outside and the wind picks up We all make phone calls to friends and families, to ensure everyone is safe and sound. It begins.

The rain starts falling much like any other rainstorm. I feel a bit more relaxed. But Katrina is still not here. She is steadily approaching and we wait and watch. The kids are busying themselves with indoor activities. Actually, the kids are all young adults or close to it. They play cards, board games and video games when they can convince us to turn off the television weather for a while. It will be a few hours, but we are getting the outer bands of weather now. The winds grow stronger. Still, I see nothing out of the ordinary. Mike and Steve piddle around the garage checking the generator. Dianne and I make breakfast, biscuits and cinnamon rolls. The food disappears in a hurry with nine hungry mouths.

The wind picks up quite a bit I see that the storm is upon us. The rain is steady but not the heavy storm I had expected. In fact, every few minutes the wind dies and it looks like a typical South Louisiana rainy day. But the wind hasn't really died down, just Mother Nature gathering a deep breath to blow more furiously the next time around. I am watching the storm more than the TV. My eyes are fixed on a pine tree outside the back glass door I say, "That pine tree looks like it might fall." Mike and the adults look out. Mike says, 'No way.' I repeat, "I'm telling you, that pine tree is going to go." Steve says, "Mary might be right, Mike." Outside the winds are increasing from the north. The actual Katrina path is slightly east of us. All of us know that the storm going to our east is good. The west side of the storm is the 'weaker' side. Anything but the east side of the storm would be better for us. Being on the west side, the winds are lashing us from the north. It seemed to me that it was almost a curving wind that lashed at us like the end of a whip would. Not a steady straight stream that sustained and then died, but a curving, unfurling current followed by a huge gust that gave the final lashing to us. As I stared at this phenomenon, the tree cracked about 15 feet up and fell to the ground I shouted, "The tree fell!" Everyone looked out but we were still unaware of the state of our lives. Mike went out the other side of the house to see what was happening. I opened the door in the back to venture outside. The power was indescribable. A small

9

overhang on columns protects the porch. I reached for the column and dared not move further away into the yard, away from safety and security of the house. I peered around the corner of the house to the other part of our property I suddenly realized that the forest behind our house was not the dark wall it used to be but that I could see fairly well through it. I saw many trees; large and small on the ground and the ones still standing were losing branches, big branches, and threatening to be next to hit the ground. I let go of the column to try to gauge the gusts as they hit. The winds push past and then die down and then another lash with a strong, steady stream, then a pause. As the stronger gusts hits me, I quickly reached for the column again afraid to be knocked over when the next gust blew me. It was at once awesome and terrifying

I returned to the house and continued to go about normal activities, trying not to focus on the danger surrounding us. The phone rings and it is a co-worker of Mike's. As I am talking to him, the phone line dies I wasn't sure what the man wanted, but now I couldn't find out. Thank goodness for cellular phones! I went to my room to lie down. Now I was a bit more concerned. I was thinking that maybe we had a small tornado that are sometimes spawned in hurricanes. Sure, that was it! Luckily it didn't hit the house. That had to be it. I tried to rest, but my heart wouldn't let me relax. Suddenly, my door burst open and Megan cries out to me, "Mom! A tree fell on your car!" I lay there stunned Mike enters the room and says it's not bad, not to worry. But I was worried - just more problems building up. I decided to look, even though I didn't want to and he was right. The tree hit my car but it was only the top of a tree that was not strapped. It was a smaller tree that didn't seem to do much damage at all. Thank goodness! I breathed easier thinking that the worst was over. How I would love to feel that way again!

The day wore on and we had to change the TV to the antenna because the satellite reception went off. Thank goodness Mike has the antenna in the attic and not outside. Another small blessing, I was finding any that I could. A small leak developed in the ceiling and we resolved the leak by putting a container in the attic to catch any water. Being indoors got to be too much for Mike. He needed to see what was going on outside as the TV showed us that the storm was upon us. He donned his hardhat, boots and a bright yellow rain slicker to go out in the storm. We jokingly referred to him as Hurricane Mike! We all teased as we saw him walk around in the back in full gear. We laughed but I was afraid, very afraid. I didn't want the kids to see my fear. I went to lay back down and listened and hoped and prayed. I prayed even harder, as I heard thump after thump and the howling winds. I thought of my loved one far away and tried to distract my mind from the present danger. My mind drifted off to my past and the beautiful moments shared, the laughter and even the struggles. I longed to let them know we were still alive and well.

The creaking and groaning continued as the house flexed in the raging and deadly wind. I return to the community area and learn more news of the storm. As the storm gets closer, she comes in contact with Lake Borne and takes an eastward jog. She stays on her northerly course and then jogs westward, then back to the northeasterly course. That little jog eastward probably saved our lives and homes. This distanced us from Katrina's center long enough to let the devastating winds lessen until she had passed by. But the danger was only beginning. We listen in horror as the news spoke of the Mississippi Gulf Coast area and the ravage there. I am surprised that there is no mention of Louisiana! After all, Katrina hit a major city, New Orleans, and the metropolitan area. Six hours after waking, it seems we are almost in the clear. I breathe easier now knowing the storm is passing and we have little damage. Or so I thought. One of our cell phone rings and it's our 'neighbor' behind us on a small gravel road called Boey Jenkins Road. His in-laws are with them and the mother-in-law's insulin needs refrigeration. They don't have a generator and need to bring the insulin over to us. Mike says he is coming over. Their house is basically cattycorner to our property. It's about 500' to the corner and then about 1400' to their road. Then it is about another 500 feet to their doorstep. Steve and Mike survey the outside and then the kids, restless with cabin fever are rounded up to help Mike cut some trees that have fallen across our road in front of the house. A few minutes later, Mike and Steve come in with grim looks on their face, "There are so many trees across the road, we might be here a while," announces Mike to the group. I am skeptical of Mike's statement. Surely he is exaggerating our status because he is in the Boy Scout survivorship mode. I brush off his prediction with the determination that I will see for myself. They leave again towards the street. I pull out my fire department slicker and boots and follow. The rain is belting and I'm hot, the air steamy and the wind still gusting. I trudge to the street to find the group following Mike to the next tree. I look at the street to the corner and see downed power lines at the corner, 500 feet away, as well as several down trees. Well, that seemed a mess, must have been a tornado, I muse.

I cry to Mike over the rain and still pulsing wind, "Stay away from those lines! And I don't like the kids around here."

"They're dead!" he shouts over the storm.

My heart is pounding fearful of the lines and the nasty damage that could create more disaster. Mike yanks the chainsaw rope and it rumbles to life as he hacks through yet another tree. As he cuts, the kids and Steve move the pieces to the side the road. I grab branches and limbs and join the team. Another tree moved, and then another. The intersection to one of our main outlets to town almost reached. Finally the third tree is moved and we come to the corner. "That wasn't too bad!" I think to myself. But there is another problem. The cross-section of power lines is stretching down and we can't drive the truck by because they cover the whole intersection. My heart is racing now as the kids and Steve cautiously avoids the lines. They are swaying in the strong Katrina winds, which are still whipping around us.

Mike yells again, "They're dead! Don't worry."

I have to trust, but Steve and I are not willing to risk the kids to chance. Together, we watch Mike plow ahead.

He steps over, then without any hesitation touches the wires to move them from his path. My heart skips a beat and then…nothing. He was right. All the lines are shut down. As I turn the corner and look down Lowe-Davis Road, I am hit with another reality, one I was not ready for, I admit. The road isn't there! I can only see trees. Trees of every size and shape, electrical poles, wires, fences, fence posts and debris block the view of a passage. There is no passage! The forest has reclaimed the land once belonging to civilization. Mike comes up to Steve and I and shuts off the saw. I just stand there stunned and crestfallen as I realize why Mike's prediction was made. There is no passage to civilization, to food, fuel, & supplies.

Steve says, "Mike there's no way we can get through all that."

I chime in, "Steve is right, there's no way!"

Our pessimism leaves Mike undeterred. He doesn't answer but pulls the cord again as the kids watch us confer. The chainsaw roars as he shouts, "We can do it! Laura's mother needs help!"

The storm rages about us and the kids and Mike set off on the first of what seemed an endless number of trees that isolate us from literally anyone. We are alone. I think both Steve and I at the same time realize that if we don't do it, no one will. Steve and I share one trait, while Mike and Dianne share the opposite trait We are the intellectuals, the thinkers. Mike and Dianne are the creative, hands-on engineers. I guess it lends truth to the adage that opposites attract. But thinking won't get us to the Munch's house, or to my parents, or to town. Only action will help us to survive. As the rain pours down and the wind blows, I stand there debating with myself at the predicament.

Steve shouts, "Mary, go get the gas and the screwdriver we left at the house."

I trudge off, still in shock and still wondering how to respond. When I come inside, I tell Dianne of the situation as I strip off my slicker and boots. My Capri jeans and t-shirt are damp with a mixture of rain and sweat. I find she has held down the fort and prepared food and drink. I give her my slicker and tell her if she wants to use it she can. It's too hot and I just don't care if I get wet anymore. I keep the boots, but I bandage my already blistering heels. I pick up the supplies and head back. I back the truck up to the corner and walk to meet the team. I am now ready to not be part of the problem, but part of the solution. We have one saw and 7 helping hands. There is Steve and I, Matthew Adam 22, Mathew Guyton, 18, Megan 19, Johnny 19, and David 16. Johnny and David smaller framed and unaccustomed to laboring in this way are showing great character and willingness. Matthew and Mathew, our boys, are more muscular. Matthew Adam is a bit clumsy and slow to respond to direction, but is able to pick up larger pieces. Mathew G., lean but strong, quietly enacts order from Mike while agilely negotiating the limbs and trees. Megan, small and attractive, but full of Tomboy never shirked a helping hand. I am proud of all of these kids. Not a grumble is heard about the work or a mutter about the conditions.

Obviously Katrina is not through with us yet as we work, the gusts push against trees still towering above us. Loose limbs and dangling broken trees threaten to be break off and crash. The gusts last from 15-25 seconds. My body shivers from the soaked clothes I wear, even though it is hot. Steve sends David and Matthew A. to get the green cart with the small generator (a spare one) on it. We will clear the road to get this generator to the Munch's house. Johnny and Mathew G. are sent to get his truck and water, as we are all losing hydration.

Still sawing and moving, the team works steadily for about four hours. Limb after limb, branch after branch, we are scratched, bumped, scraped, snagged and tripped. We only stop to watch any tree that seems threatening to fall. In the distance, through the branches we spot our neighbor's daughter, Melissa. She negotiates through the web towards us "Dad is using his saw on Boey Jenkins," she informs us. Our team just got bigger by two volunteers, Bill and his son Michael Munch. At this point, we have turned from Lowe-Davis Road onto Boey Jenkins and a final pine tree blocks the Munches driveway With energy we didn't think was still in us, we watched the saw rip through it and all of us rolled the huge log to the side of the drive. A great cheer went up from our team and the Munch family watching us from the garage. It was the first good feeling I had had all day! I look at Mike as he shuts off the saw and sits nearby on the tailgate. He looks completely worn. The chainsaw has sucked the energy from him and he is gearing up for renewed strength. If you have never handled a chainsaw, you cannot know the power it takes just to wield it. It is a wonderful time saving tool, but it takes constant grip, pressure, and control to manage the machine. It's heavy, because he has a large blade. Using it can wipe a younger man out in an hour or less. As I watch him, I am concerned that he is pushing himself too much. I'm glad he is taking a moment to rest.

As we walk in the garage, Laura hands us all dry towels. But some of our group heads to the back yard. In a minute or two, after Mike sets to work on getting the generator started, those from the backyard beckon me to join them. They have jumped in the pond back there. Still shivering from the dampness and covered with sawdust and wood particles, the invitation is too good to pass up. I wade cautiously in the pond as the young people and Steve jump right in. In seconds, we are laughing and splashing in the warm muddy pond water as if it were a day at the beach. The water smells like the mud it covers, the heavy odor of clay and soil mixing with the water, fresh from the rain. I remember my youth as I wade in. As kids, we used to swim in the bayou at my Aunt's house and we played endless hours in our own pond covered in mud. The temperature of the water varies and you feel warm and cool spots as you swim. The bottom is soft and mucky. My boots dig in and the suction makes my foot pull free of the boot that is stuck there. I can wriggle it free well enough to maneuver to the deeper area of the pond. I duck my head under to feel the fresh water wash my hair free of the sawdust and sweat. It feels great! I laugh as we all enjoy this rustic moment and I feel like a kid again! As we all get out, for just a few moments,

I didn't think of the troubles or problems that may lie ahead. I just treasured a few minutes of mindless fun.

As I enter the garage, the generator is rumbling to a start Mike did what he had set out to do. Now the Munch's will be able to keep the insulin refrigerated. Tired and soaked, we say our good-byes after a few minutes of exchanging stories, and we all jump in the bed of the truck as Mathew weaves his way to our house in the rabbit path we cleared from the road.

When we come in, we all shower in cold water and then gathered in the den for the dinner with the food I had prepared the day before. Some had red beans and rice, while others had beef roast. Dianne had set up everything and now we bowed our heads to pray and give thanks for our lives, our safety and our good fortune to have our home spared. We were all ravenous and tired, but content and safe. It was now time for a meeting of the minds and a call to order for the realities we face. Mike called the parents together and we sat in the living room as the kids played cards after dinner.

"It looks like we might be here for a while together. The roads are completely blocked and it will be a while before we have power. I think it could be as much as a month," stated Mike.

"We need to take stock of what we have and make some rules," I agreed.

I didn't think we would be stranded for a month, but I knew it could be a long while. I didn't have an estimated time frame in my head. I wanted to plan for the worse and hope for the best. After a short discussion among ourselves, we gathered the two families together. We laid out the realities and the plan for the kids. The Dads would be in charge of work details, duties, power usage and correction. The Dads instructed the young people that the Moms would prepare meals, and allocate meal times, refrigerator use, water use, and other household issues. Effective immediately, no one would open the refrigerator without express permission. Bathrooms were assigned and air mattresses, beds and couches were allocated to individuals. It was explained that there are many personalities to deal with and that we had to respect each other and as moods come and go, separate yourself if need be. We tried to present ourselves with calm and confidence and not to over emphasize the peril but convey the reason for concern. Of course, the youth seemed to think we were overreacting, but we told them we would rather err on the side of caution than to be caught with no food or water a week down the road.

Mike, Steve Dianne and I met again on the food supply, which was good, and the power supply, which was excellent. Fuel would become an issue fairly soon unless we changed generators. Mike and I had plastic totes with extra canned food, toilet paper, towels, lighters, fuel, bags, soap, toothpaste, and much more. Our pantry was full, our freezer stocked fairly well and we had one thing many people didn't have – Electricity! We checked guns and ammo for safety purposes. I never thought we would have to think of protecting ourselves this way, but to be sure, we needed to think ahead and be prepared. I guess it is good that there was a house full of Boy Scouts of Eagle rank to act on the Boy Scout motto, "Be prepared." Mike, Matthew, Mathew and Johnny are all Eagle Scouts. Steve wasn't an Eagle Scout but had been involved in Scouting with his sons for over 15 years and had been on many high adventure trips all over the country with Mike and the boys. I felt secure that these men would know how to help us survive even without the conveniences we now had. As I lay my head on my pillow this night, I am exhausted from the grueling day, but I couldn't sleep. I have never felt like this before. I felt secure in our plans, but unsure of our futures. I felt this was a life-changing event and that, not only would our area of the world change, but we would too.

Day 1 - Aftermath (Tuesday 8/30/05)

We are up early and Dianne and I prepared breakfast bacon, sausage and the remainder of the biscuits. Mike and Steve bring the Boy Scout bus around to the house driveway. The bus, owned jointly by the Scariano's and us, is a huge 38-passenger 1963 Eagle (similar to a Greyhound type). The bus has a huge generator on board that runs the A/C for the bus. Mike wants to use this diesel generator to power the house. We also have a 15 kw generator outside that Mike wants to change over to later on. He said it would run the A/C at least to half the house. It is already hot in the house. We set up fans around the main living area and used the ceiling fans. We work on the laundry from all the dirty clothes from yesterday, and hang them on the cable Mike strung up for us outside. The dryer is too much of a draw on electricity. Then the men rounded up the boys and fired up the chainsaw to try to go the other way on our street towards the other outlet to town and to the Scariano's house. Megan was offered to go on the work detail or to stay with us and plan the meals for the next several days. She chose to work on the chainsaw gang. I walked outside a bit later and found that several other neighbors had joined our work force and the sawing was in full swing. By midday, they had made it to a large open part of the street where no trees had fallen. Hope for rescue seemed to grow. But Mike told me later that the main highway to town, Hwy 435, was nearly as bad as Lowe Davis. I felt my hopefulness turn the corner to doubt. The ever-changing emotions that accompany each turn of events pulls here and there like a July 4th Tug-o-war. I try to keep a balanced approach regardless.

The group returns and the men tinker with the generator after lunch. The bus generator gives us lots of options for power. It works great! I wondered about my family members and friends. The TV is constantly on for the latest happenings in our part of the world. We are seeking the status of our families and the areas they lived in, and for many, the outlook was bleaker than our own. New Orleans, city of my birth and home to many friends and family, is underwater! Flooding pours in to the below-sea level city, the city that care forgot. The water came after the storm. Hurricanes produce storm surge. The water in front of the storm is pushed inland as the storm forges ahead; much like the action made when your hand is half in, half out of the water and you move it from one point to another. The storm surge is high and powerful. The New Orleans levee system was not able to hold with that tremendous power. There are at least two levee breaches on canals that aid in protecting the city from flooding. The levees are designed to withstand up to a Category 3 storm. But many years of no funding and/or empty promises for improvements probably meant they couldn't withstand a Cat 3. Indeed, I believe Katrina was stronger than the Category 3 she was dubbed. The first breech is on the Industrial Canal, which is a navigable, man-made waterway that provides a shorter route between the Gulf and the River (as opposed to following the River all the way to the mouth). The second breach is on the 17th Street Canal on the New Orleans side This breech is near enough to my father-in-law's house in Lakeview that we could conclude that his house had to be underwater. I look at Mike as we learn of this, but I see no emotion, just plain resignation to the facts. We all shake our heads in disbelief and shock. We had no words but only grief and confusion over what the future held. Steve works at Loyola, Mike at the Port of New Orleans. Our livelihoods are heavily dependent on the city. What would that mean? We had no idea now. We also had no phones. The lines were dead. Our cellular service was gone too, no power to the towers and antenna blown down. We were on an island with no contact to our friends and families who we wanted to check on, or who we wanted to let know that we were okay. It is extremely frustrating and stressful not knowing and not being able to let others know our status. We had no way to contact my in-laws to give them comfort and support for anything they might need. We had a window to the world from the TV, but we had no way to reach the world.

My parents live two miles down the road. That afternoon, Mike and Steve decide to walk through the Lowe-Davis trees to check on my parents. They make it there and back but it took a long time on foot and crossing all that debris. Mike's predictions about clearing the roads seemed right. My parents are okay and they have my sister, Lori, my brother (Ellis) and his wife, my niece and a family friend. A tree has fallen on the pump house and though they had a generator, they have no fresh water. Our goal tomorrow is to bring them plenty of water. They have an in-ground swimming pool to use for washing and flushing water, and they had put up fresh water before the storm (a normal drill for most people here when storms threaten). Everyone was safe and the house was intact. Many very large trees had fallen; one only inches away.

Tonight we bow our heads again after a busy day. Our thanks are for more news of our loved ones, the continued safety of our household, and for the food and water in plenty. The kids are in good spirits and play cards or video games. It is our second night in our 'storm prison.' I believe I am still dazed at this point from the news reports. I always knew New Orleans was in danger. We often have spoken of the 'bowl effect' and the catastrophe awaiting the city should a strong storm threaten. Here it is happening. It doesn't seem real, but like a dream. But what was happening to New Orleans is different than what is happening to us. Our present crisis is first and foremost on our minds, though we still sympathized with those in the city. The TV news has reports from all over and the reporters constantly repeating, "We have no news from the St. Tammany Parish area, no one has reported from there." I want to scream at them…."You idiots! We have no phones! No power! No nothing! How can we let you know? Send help!" I hear them say the same for at least three days. It seems to me, somebody should have tried to find out, but I quickly realize, nothing was as it should be because we all were suffering.

Tonight, when I talk to Mike, we both realize that he has no job, and I have no job and it could last a long time. I feel scared and still stunned that this is all happening. Mike works at the Port of New Orleans. It is becoming clear that the city was no longer viable and even though I am skeptical of initial predictions, even my best guess was unemployment for at least a month. How would we manage? For the first time, I felt helplessly out of control of my life and had a sense of despair that I quickly tried to suppress. I cried that night. It was the first time I had a chance to release the fear and hopelessness. I wasn't giving up, but I needed to let my emotions explode or I would have more stress than I could handle. Katrina would claim more victims than those that lost life, home or property through water and wind. She was costing our jobs and thus our homes and property through economic hardship. I don't think I was alone in my sorrow, but if others were dejected, they hid it from view. I hid much from the children. As parents, I guess it's a normal reaction, to keep the kids protected from our burdens.

Day 2 - (Wednesday 8/31/05)

As I wake, I realize that I'm not dreaming. The morning air is heavy and the hum of the fan tells me before I open my eyes that we are still in our situation. No one can work. We can't drive anywhere and no one can drive to us. I come in to prepare breakfast and wash one load of clothes. Mike comes in shortly to announce that Hwy 435 is cleared and that he has found a way at least to my parents' house. The way in to Abita Springs (a nearby small town) is blocked by rising floodwater from the Abita River. The boys, Steve and Mike load up camping water containers from the Boy Scout equipment. We wash one load each day and hang out the clothes to dry. The dryer is too much draw on the generator. We are running quite a few things even so and we are hot, but able to provide for the mainstays of life, food, water and shelter. The fans help to circulate the air and give us a breeze. Dianne and I secure a screen to the open back door to keep out the ever-pesky and present insects, especially the mosquito. We have a ceiling fan and two portable fans in the main den/kitchen area. Each bedroom has a ceiling fan and there is another portable fan in the living room where Dianne and Steve sleep. I am now getting acclimated to the dampness and moisture of my skin in this heat even with the fans and in a state of rest. Any physical activity at all produces pouring perspiration. It matters not, there is much to do; we cannot dwell on physical inconveniences and dreams of past luxuries.

When they return, Mike informs me that my Dad's generator is out and he won't accept our spare generator. I drive over to their house, now about 5 miles longer than normal because of the blocked roads and I am shocked at what I see in my country neighborhood. For the first time, I have ventured out and my heart sinks when I get a glimpse of the problems. I weave my car through a small trail dodging cut trees, down wires and other hazards. There is not enough room for two cars, but it doesn't matter because there are very few, if any, cars on the road anyway. On the main highway, in two places, there is high water that flows across the road. That is not unusual, but added to the forest that is now our road; it makes it even more difficult. I finally reach my parent's house and they are all out on the front porch.

I tell my Dad, "Why don't you want Mike to hook up our generator?"

"Awww we don't need it, we'll be alright," he states calmly, seemingly unaffected.

"Dad, what about your refrigerator and freezers? At least you can run that!" I counter.

"Ok, then," says Dad.

I'm not sure why he didn't want our help. Maybe he didn't realize the extent of the situation, or maybe he was too stubborn. In either case, I was very glad he finally relented.

I talk a few minutes more and then return home to tell Mike and the boys to load up the generator and hook it up. My Dad rides with me and I return with them all while we get them going. I feel better that they at least have food and fresh water on hand.

Mike, Steve and a group then leave us all and venture in to Abita to see the Scariano house in town. The group sets out with ice chests down Hwy435 towards the Scariano house When they approach the Abita River, it is flowing over the road, which is not out of the ordinary for heavy rains. But it is definitely impassable, Mike and Dianne stay with the truck, while the rest float the ice chests over the high water and wade through. Their house is about two or three blocks from this point. They walk the ice chests to the house. The house is dark and has a number of trees that have fallen on it. The freezer and refrigerator are emptied into either the ice chest or the garbage. The group returns and wades back with the chests and Socks, the Scariano cat in his animal carrier, much traumatized by the storm. Dianne learns that her house is damaged but only in the attic area upstairs from what can be seen.

When the group returns, the four elders meet alone. The revised plan is to bring water to my parents every other day and also to make it to the Scariano house and retrieve some belongings and a few food items tomorrow. We also have to make plans to remove the trees and weatherize their house. We have found that some of our gas cans are missing and Mike reported that several neighbors have missing guns and other items. Mike demands that there be someone at home all the time and preferably two people. I retrieve my 357 Magnum and pull out my ammunition. Since Dianne and I are usually the sentries at the house, I prepare myself both physically and mentally. I didn't want to be caught off guard should the time in our exile grow and people become desperate. I also show Dianne how to use the pistol and where I am keeping it. There are other weapons in the house if needed. I didn't like to think that it would come to this, but after hearing of looting in the city and with many people everywhere without resources, we had to be prepared. I prayed that we would not have to resort to violence to protect ourselves and survive.

Also in our plans, we decide to send Mathew G., Megan, and Johnny to Baton Rouge to buy gas. Reports on the news state that even Baton Rouge is short on fuel because of the excessive demand. One thing is sure - there is no fuel nearby. On the way, they will also go to Megan's apartment in Hammond and empty any contents that they can carry. She has not moved home and still needs to accomplish this before long.

We gather for dinner and because we are living in such close quarters, edginess and irritability are inevitable. Dianne and I have conspired to give out a reward. It is a contest for a candy prize. No one knows what is being measured. The first person to compliment the dinner or meal will get a Reese's candy. As we serve ourselves and sit down to eat after our prayer, Mathew G. says the first compliment on the meal. He wins! We all laugh and try to make the best of our living situation and predicament. Steve comes up with a wonderful exercise in goodwill. After we eat, we each must say something nice about the person next to us. We each take turns speaking our feelings, positively about each other. It turns out that this makes us think positively and troubles tend to dissipate quickly. The kids protest about this game, but Steve is persistent. Steve says each night we will do this and he will create the order and you can't talk about the same person and you have to say something different. It helped ease the tension and stress. We all benefited from this game and even learned a few things about each other and ourselves from it.

One night, it was my turn. It so happens that Mike was sitting next to me and I had to comment on him according to the order set by Steve. Others had talked about how a person was nice or helpful or many other things. I turned to Mike and as I looked at him I realized that everyone knows that I love him as my husband. I searched for the right words to describe my feelings and my mouth spoke before my brain could stop me from being shy, "You're my hero." There was a quiet pause as everyone realized what I said. He didn't say anything, but his eyes softened as he looked at me. In that moment, no words were necessary between us. The flash of his saving work, his determination to help the neighbors, his insistence on getting to my parents', his taking control of our situation, and in helping our friends by housing them all came together in one sentence. Of course, then everyone chimes in with "Awwwwww, ohhhhhhhh, how mushy!" But I meant it. I don't think I have meant anything more in my life.

It is hot. The fan blows across my body as I lay on top of the sheets hoping to cool off some. Tonight as I lay my head down after having watched the unfolding realization of the devastation and trouble, I feel that we are luckier than most, but I'm deeply troubled and in a state of shock, I know. I drift off to sleep dreaming of better days in the past with loving but distant friends and family. They don't know what has happened to us, no one does. I want so badly to make contact with that world, but the communication infrastructure is gone. We cannot connect to the outside world. The outside world doesn't care about us.

Day 3 -Thursday (9/1/05)

The day starts out badly for me. The 3 young people left on their quest for gas, but not without warnings and cautions about not stopping, being cautious and using good judgment. Silently I ask their Guardian Angels to keep them safe. As I prepare an old Southern favorite, Pain Perdue, more commonly known as French Toast, the stress level seems to have Mike on a power trip and I am determined that Dianne be able to view the damage to her house. After all, Dianne and I have been cooped up in the house for three days! The tensions rise as Mike and I begin our dispute about Dianne and I leaving the house today. Our friends sit by as the discord breaks out between Mike and me. It became a spectacle in absurdity. I am humiliated and ashamed that he acts the way he does sometimes. It's more than I can stand and I snap like the many trees pressed beyond their limits by the Katrina gusts. Now that we have the roads clear, I feel the need to leave. I've never felt like this before. I start gathering my things, not knowing exactly how, but thinking maybe I could get away to St.Louis to my cousin's house for a while; anywhere but here, in the heat and in his line of fire. Dianne tries to talk to me, but I am determined, crying and broken. I don't know what

Dianne is struggling with but finally in frustration, she burst into tears. I am surprised.

"Mary you can't leave! If you leave, I have to leave too!" she cries.

In an instant, we embrace trying to give each other comfort. I think it was a manifestation of the stress that pervades our lives now. After about an hour, I sit down with her on my bed and we both cry, talk and deepen our friendship and attempt to grasp the mysteries of marriage. Under the ceiling fan, we neglect the morning's laundry and chores to gain perspective on our current situation. Sometime later, Mike comes in and is apologetic and wants to resolve this. I only commit to making it through our current crisis before making any decisions about our future. I know that I shouldn't rush into judgment under these circumstances. That is what I tell him and we leave it at that. I am unafraid now and more determined than ever to get through this if only to eliminate the pressure building on all of us that compounds the ever-present problems in our lives.

The Munches show up at the house and announce that they are leaving. Laura's mother needs to fill her prescriptions and they will go to Baton Rouge with their adult children. They bring some frozen food over to put in the freezer We give our good-byes and promise to watch out for their house and keep them posted on happenings.

Somehow Mike finds out that the Home Depot has opened Mike, Steve, David and Matthew G spend the day at my parent's house fixing the water pump. The other kids return in the late afternoon with the much-needed fuel. What a relief! We will be able to manage now. They were unable to retrieve Megan's things because she forgot her key! Mathew had someone in Baton Rouge approach him and offer to buy one of our gas cans for $50! (Just the can, no fuel!) People are desperate and it's starting to be dangerous. They acted prudently and refused. I'm so happy to see them safely home. We had to send them, but I worried anyway. The world is upside down now and nothing is safe and trustworthy.

We eat dinner together as usual Tonight we sing 'Happy Birthday' to Mike What a celebration! My heart is not in it, but I make the best of it anyway I have to hold up my end of the bargain.

The four adults meet this evening and Mike brings his flashlight. We are going on a drive. We make it to town (Abita) and Dianne and I see her house for the first time. It's hard to see at night, but there are two trees laying across each other on the front of the roof. The other trees have collapsed the roof over the upstairs attic room. Luckily the house looks livable. There is water through to the downstairs, but fairly minimal compared to some other houses we have seen. Tomorrow, Mike and the crew will begin work on their house to remove the trees.

Day 4 - (Friday 9/2/05)

Each and every day we watch the growing problems in New Orleans; the people on rooftops, the rescues by boat and helicopter. The media is making news frenzy about the FEMA delayed response. We don't see that. We see a national and even worldwide response and growing. We see that, just like us, the storm was seemingly harmless and came suddenly to deadly force in the blink of an eye. My perspective is that neighbors and friends and local communities help each other and ourselves. Here, we don't sit around and wait for solutions, but find our own. Even my step-brother-in-law, who was in New Orleans in the rising water, found a way out, not waiting to be rescued. Then there were the ever-present racial issues created by the media. My friend, Katrina knows no colors and no lifestyle. She sweeps up all of the trash and treasure alike as she blows by. The poor are not in low areas and the rich are not in high areas, nor are the black in low areas and the white in high areas. Rich, poor, black, white, Asian, Hispanic, any and all people suffered. Any and all people lost houses, jobs, businesses, loved ones. The suffering is wide and plenty. It agonizes me to see stories told that miss the point entirely.

Today, we are all exhausted and Steve declares a day off. We start to pick up branches and debris in the yard while Mike and Steve go to the Scariano's and to the only store operating in the entire area encompassing three towns. After just an hour or so, it is so hot we all came inside. The kids talked about cooling off in the down-the-street neighbor's pool. Finally, I agree that they could run down there and swim. The neighbors had evacuated but since Megan and Mathew are related to them and have given them an open-door invitation to swim, I thought it would be okay. Off they ran and they enjoyed the cool and leisure. When Mike returned, he surprises us by putting the small window unit in the den area. We close the doors to the other half the house (with my bedroom on that side) and hang a sheet at the kitchen opening to the laundry/bedroom area. This little luxury brings back the things I had taken for granted in the time before Katrina. We are all delighted! Lights, air conditioning, and even cooking and refrigeration are not given second thoughts each and every day. When you are limited or without these daily, it becomes an enormous value to be able to experience these things again. I reflected on people throughout the world to whom these things are unknown! I flavor a small taste of their challenges and I thank the Good Lord for our many blessings even without the modern conveniences. I also begin to realize that we play a part in having these blessings by not waiting for handouts. We struggle by the sweat of our brow and dedication to achieve a higher standard. Even though many are in our same situation, there are those who choose to sit and cry over and those who choose to take action and work for better things. This A/C brings another issue into play. Now everyone wants to sleep in the den. The two queen air mattresses are less than adequate for all. I defer to them and elect to stay in my bed with my fan. I have grown accustomed to the balmy breeze and once I take a colder-than-wanted shower, my body is cool enough to allow me to fall asleep with the hum of the portable fan. What keeps me awake is the anxiety, not the temperature.

The kids play video games and board games. It is fun to watch them, as they seem carefree. They banter and challenge and tease. I join in a vigorous game of Egyptian Ratsu. We all laugh and joke at how fast Megan slaps the doubles that are laid down. The day is relaxing and we had a wonderful treat for dinner. Mathew G had fished in Grand Isle some weeks earlier and we had some frozen Red Fish that we put on the BBQ pit. That fish was fantastic! You would think we were living in luxury from the things that we could scrape up for meals.

I have the opportunity to drive in to town today. I went in search of phone line for email and news of other family. The drive is difficult, but somewhat improved over my first outing to my parents' home. The trees still cover the road to the extent that only one car could pass all the way to Abita. After getting to the main commercial area in Covington, the streets open up because no trees line this main six-lane highway close enough to cause blockage. I learn that my brother's house has phone service. Strangely, the phone line allows me to use my computer, but I still couldn't call phone numbers and get through. I use his house today and each day for my fix to link to the outside world. I have to break in to his house most days because he was working overtime with the Fire Dept. He knows about it, so no problem. Dianne and I seek information and file claims with insurances, FEMA and unemployment. Our discovery opens many doors closed to most in our situation, with the communication infrastructure so damaged and destroyed all over the parish. There seemed to be few cars out on the road.

The feeling was that the entire area was still reeling from the blow it had been dealt, like a punch to the stomach. When will we stagger forward and catch our breath?

Dianne and I also find the FEMA location where they are distributing MRE (Meals Ready-to-Eat), water and ice. We learn of the Red Cross food distribution times and locations. We make use of these when the chainsaw crew is working at the Scariano's to remove the trees. The towns are ghost towns. There are no traffic lights, no stores are open with only two exceptions, Home Depot and Save-A-Center, which had opened this day for the first time and only for a few hours. They have little staff and are running a generator to run the cash registers. There is only one Oil Company opening with gas, Shell Gas is such a precious commodity, they have posted a guard at each entrance and direct cars to pumps and limit the amount purchased. The lines are long. We don't bother with those lines now. We have our cars full and our cans/barrels full too. We are okay for now.

It was a productive first day out I feel a small stirring in the community. Mainly what we see is heavy machinery starting to roll in. Prior to this, people had cleared the roads. People like us with chainsaws and tractors. People who decided to take matters into their own hands. I don't think public workers did any actual clearing. They only moved the cut trees back to open the roads wider. It was inspiring to think of how much we can accomplish as friends, neighbors and nearby strangers.

At our parent meeting this night, it is decided that Steve and Mathew G. would drive as far as necessary to buy diesel for the bus generator. I objected to this because I felt we should start on the Scariano house soon. We could drive in to Abita now and we needed to secure their house. Steve and Mike overruled my objections in favor of more fuel.

As I reflect on the upheaval of my life, I'm not sure it will ever be the same. I know it will be a long while before it even resembles the normality we once had. In some ways, it is a taste of our most basic response, that of survival. In other ways, it is frightening to the point of being drained of hope. The emotional collapse of the inner strength stands a breath away at times, like nearing a cliff and feeling as though a slight breeze might send you over the side. It evokes simultaneous reactions of running to find safety and daring to push further to the brink to taste danger more fully in order to value life more deeply. The uncertainty of our future is the only certainty.

Day 5 - Saturday (9/3/05)

Today Matthew A. leaves to go to Mississippi to see his maternal grandfather who is close to death from cancer. Matthew will be gone about three days. He has suffered the hurricane, the loss of his uncle and now his grandfather. During the storm, his uncle died of a massive heart attack at a young age. I hope Matthew will be able to cope I'm glad he is able to go to his grandfather one last time.

Steve and Mathew G. head out to find diesel in the afternoon. After visiting with some relatives to check on the status of people and checking emails at my brother's house, we attend vigil mass at St. Jane's with no air conditioning and few people. In a church that holds over 400 people, there are only about 50 people in attendance. I give thanks to our Lord for our many blessings. There is a depth of prayer that transcends everyone's normal offerings. It is a quiet and meaningful prayer for our own community that is suffering. The mass is abbreviated because of the heat. Although all the windows are open, with only candlelight, it is still a sacrifice. We are surprised to see Dianne and Steve at mass. Steve and Mathew G. found diesel in Hammond (30 miles) and with that good luck, we think we are set. But we are mistaken! The bus generator gave out this night. That means the diesel run was in vain, at least for our purposes now. We revert back to the small generator and lost some of the outlets and lights we previously had. We also lost the microwave or traded microwave power for some other power. But at least we have power. I feel blessed anyway.

Day 6 (Sunday 9/4/05)

The day starts normally, at least as normal as we can expect. Megan is visiting at my parents' home. Mom and Megan decide to bike ride to my house. They come in for a short visit then leave to ride back. Suddenly I see a four-wheeler in the back yard. I grab my gun cautiously making it available. Dianne is walking the dog in the back and speaks to the rider briefly. She comes in to tell me my mom has fallen off her bike. I drive to them about

700 feet away around the corner. My mom is bleeding really badly and her head is swollen. Megan and I get her in the car and I say I'm taking her to the ER. My heart is pounding wildly I am trying to make reasonable decisions considering that NOTHING was normal now. I decide to pick up my Dad (a retired physician) because I have no way to call him now or later with no phone service. I know that every minute counts with a head trauma, but consider that she is conscious and talking and decide to go the extra two minutes out of the way to get him I drive to their house and he rides with me to St. Tammany hospital. My sister follows us in her own truck. My brother Ellis and his wife Shannon meet us there. At first, all is well. But because of her age, they want to observe her for a while. She is 69. About two hours later, (around 9:00 PM) the hospital is unable to locate a neurologist to read the CT scan.

The nurse asks Mom, "Do you know what today is?"

Mom says " It's the 23rd Sunday in Ordinary Time."

To most people that might seem wrong. But in actuality, according to the Catholic year, she is right! We laugh outside the ER, but I know that Mom is losing coherence and starting to say other odd responses. It is decided that I will go their house to stay the night with their last houseguest, Margaret Claiborne. I stop by my house to tell them the status and then go to their home. About an hour later, Ellis and Shannon show up at my parents' house. They tell me that Mom is being transported to Baton Rouge. Her condition has worsened and they are unable to contact a neurologist. She is having seizures. When I hear this, I feel myself shiver with a fear of unknown and my strong façade dissipates into tears at what this might mean. How much more can I stand emotionally? I know the Lord will support me and I naturally lift my mind and spirit in a quick prayer that helps me to gather myself together. As it happens, my brother Chris is at the ER in the ambulance and requests permission to transport. My Dad goes with her. I go with Ellis to Baton Rouge. Shannon stops by my house to tell them I am in Baton Rouge. In Baton Rouge, David and Rachel are there with Rachel's sister, Rebecca. Rachel and David are staying with Rachel's family in Baton Rouge during all of the storm reconstruction. About 2 AM, they have stabilized my mother and are moving her to ICU. There's not much more I can do, and hanging around seems pointless. We leave my Dad (and the things we brought for him from the house) and return home I come home about 330 AM. I am exhausted and yet restless. Now I have this to deal with and I'm upset, but I know my mother is in good hands. Our Lady of the Lake Hospital is an excellent facility.

Monday - (Labor Day) Week two begins

The group begins work on the Scariano house. We trade off staying at home during the day to prevent looting. During this week, I finally see the towns stretch and yawn as they wake from the slumber of shock and unconsciousness that had left everyone stunned and reeling. I see Covington has restored some power to the commercial downtown area. Then I see that some of the businesses on Hwy190 areas are emerging as well. Each day I try to make it to my brother's to get online to check claims, check bank accounts, contact family and friends and let them know our status. I laugh as Steve starts calling the kids his "Little Ducks" as they become part of the tree workers.

Each day the working boys/men are getting food from the Red Cross relief truck. Mike starts his own crew of removing trees from houses. Every day, people approach them as they see them taking trees off houses. The boys are paid by the hour and Mist LLC is now in a new line of work Mike, Steve, Mathew G, Johnny and David are an efficient working crew that removes at least a tree a day. They are making some money and that is good since no one is able to return to work. Mike ingeniously uses block & tackle and straps and cables to lift the trees without the use of heavy machinery. I am quite impressed by many things about this. First, his role as provider for our family has spurred him to be creative in using his God-given abilities to earn money to help with the expenses. Secondly, he possesses an innate creative, mechanical know-how that still mystifies me, and probably the majority of people who do not possess that know-how. It's much like the sculptor who sees his finished artwork while it is still a block of clay. I cannot even delve into the concepts that he knows, but it astounds me even after all these years. Lastly, I see the happiness and relief to the people he helps, even though they are paying him, he is fair with his prices, unlike so many of those workers who descended upon our community to make their fortune instead of giving aid and comfort. Besides, Mike and Steve did several jobs at no cost for those who had absolutely no means of paying for it or without insurance. I am proud of this man because at the root of it all, he really just likes helping other people if he can. It's good to know that they can help.

Tuesday comes and that night the Scariano's, who live in the Town of Abita, get power restored to their home. The trees are off and the breach in the roof is covered. They return to their home to live. Our kids stay with them in the air conditioning. I decide to stay with my home. I need to begin the work to get my home back in order. I feel more comfortable being surrounded by my own things, in my own bed. I cling to this almost as if I would lose everything like so many others were I to even so much as blink. I see so much loss, so much sorrow. Sure, people lives were saved and that is truly the main thing. But their lives are now so changed; it strikes to the core of their being. The responses to this are as varied as the individual, but it is nonetheless as sorrowful as the death of a loved one. It is not the material things that people mourn, but the life, memories, and structure that those things represent. It is their security, livelihoods, and familiarity that surrounded them and kept them safe and in control. Now they must sink down in their sorrow and hopefully rise to find their pioneering spirit and move on.

During this week, I am surprised at the army of utility workers, tree and restoration trucks, fire and emergency personnel that are present. The helicopters are an ever-present, common site nowadays. They land in Covington bringing various supplies and video taping the area. I've seen many C-130's in the air probably with supplies, and some that were re-fueling helicopters in flight. I have seen and met people from Virginia, Oklahoma, Alabama, New York, Maryland, Oklahoma, Arkansas, Texas and many more places. It's feels like someone stepped on an ant pile and now the ants are scurrying to re-build their mound. In many ways, it is that way.

The news reports of evacuations from the city are almost not worth mentioning since most of it is political spin or mass hysteria. One city counsel woman shouts to reporters "If you want to help, send busses and gas." As the reporters try to ask more questions, she repeats over 8 times, "Busses and gas, we need busses and gas, give us busses and gas." We all laugh until we cry about idiocy of this 'politician.' She is pulling up her sleeves and getting to work, but begging for handouts! It is that welfare mentality that has crippled New Orleans so severely, not the poverty or race or even bureaucratic tardiness. It is the mental state of mind that is ingrained in many of those in the Superdome or the Convention Center that sit there and wait till the government comes to GIVE THEM SOMETHING. It can be anything, but by God, I'll not lift a finger to help myself. We discuss how much better things would have been if it had been like the old days of Civil Defense. Each local area had a designated certified shelter and small groups would be in each with local deputies of the Civil Defense who had training in disasters in charge. It is folly to think any organization or law enforcement can handle tens of thousands of hysterical people, lost people, and sick/injured people and expect order and propriety. With small groups, it is manageable and there is accountability. It would also help to have these people in the city once the storm is passed to help with organizing groups for clean-up in their own areas. It would also have helped with rescue to have small groups in designated shelters so that all would be gathered in one place and plans to move could be practiced or prepared in the event of rising water. All that would be too sensible! Small groups would not be allowed to do the damage and have the squalor because you would know most of those present from your neighborhood, and secondly because the Civil Defense team would have drills on keeping sanitary conditions. The Superdome's damage by the wind is one factor, but the bigger ruin is from the sheltered people who showed total disregard for anything. It is sad and shameful. I do not feel sorry for those who acted that way. Poverty should not be an excuse for squalid living.

Steve, Dianne and I wrote a silly song about the problems everywhere. It goes as follows:

Katrina blew in and washed New Orleans out
People in the Dome, but we shipped 'em all out.
Convention Center rapin', city-wide lootin'.
Cops & military come in a-shootin'.

People on the rooftops
People in the street,
Lookin' for a meal
Ready to eat.

Throw the trash here,
Throw the trash there
Take a dump, where you want,
Doesn't matter where.

Gotta get out, gotta get out now!
What do we need? Busses & Gas!
Busses & gas, busses & gas
Bust yo ass for busses & gas!

Murphy Oil Refin'ry
Forgot to cap the well.
Now St. Bernard parish
Look like Hell!

We were lookin' for wisdom,
Someone in the know.
What did we get?
A Big Blank-O!

Wanna house in da woods,
A sweet hide-a-way?
Now dere's a tree in it
And you can see da light of day!

Had a camp for fishin'
And we love to hunt duck.
Nuttin' lef but da pilins'
And de mud and de muck.

Wanna start over,
Gonna take dat Fema check,

Gonna Get my Fema trailer,
And run like heck!

Week 3 begins

On Monday, September 12th , a full two weeks after Katrina, we have power restored. I am tired of living on a generator and the cost of gas and the amount of gas is draining us. I can finally take a shower in hot water. I see the steam rise and as I get in I shiver. It is delightful and I revel in the steam and warmth for a long time. I take my time and treat myself to the luxury of water and warmth as if it were rich chocolate or silky sheets. There are other niceties I had forgotten about. It's like a treat to be able to wash clothes and dry them. I have built up a large amount of dirty clothes and was at the point of making a laundry mat run, if I could find one open.

I have given my resignation at work because I feel the need to be at home and care for my mother, my in-laws, and our own home. I need to help the kids figure out their lives and provide guidance to them as they regain their independence. I was not satisfied with that position to begin with, and this storm made it an easy break for me.

Mike should be able to return to work fairly soon. The Port of New Orleans is vital to the commerce of this city and the country. The port opened already and is calling back workers. Mike should be called very soon. He is providing more than enough by his ingenuity and productivity in the tree business. Many people call on him and trust him to get the job done right. I wish he would put as much effort in all aspects of his life as he does in his work.

My mother returned to the area, but is staying with a friend who has power. She is recovering well. I had visited her about every other day in Baton Rouge. I couldn't afford the gas or the time away from home for more than that. No worry, I have other siblings who filled in the gaps. I am so happy she is recovering so well. She is bruised over a large part of her left side but has no broken bones. I am astounded at her health and vigor! I need to get on the vitamins she takes!

Week 4 begins - Monday Sept 19th.

I have spoken to my in-laws. Their lives are now completely different. Their house is still underwater. I was very upset by their decision to stay in the Shreveport area. After talking to Geri, my step-mother-in-law, I find that they are now in a house, fully furnished with dishes and all, for a $300/month rent. They have nearby drugstores, grocery store, bank and church. There is a Heart Hospital and a local cardiologist who has seen Mr. Edgar and renewed his prescriptions. I realize that I am being selfish in wanting them to come with us and return to this area. We have plans now to salvage their home and their rental property. We will assist them to whatever level is necessary in weeks to come.

(Saturday 9/17/05)

We went with the Scariano's to Steve's brother's business in Kenner. We toured around Metairie and Kenner and I have a new perspective on our situation. Each and every home, business, or public building was damaged in these areas. The mere scope of it is overwhelming! And this isn't the really severely destroyed parts of town. This area is considered having little damage! I have never seen this kind of devastation before. As we drive, each and every home has cleared out carpet, furniture, walls, cabinets and has piled up debris on the curb. Walls of apartment buildings are caved in. Every billboard is blown down. Silt and sand cover the flooded areas. Trees are fallen in yards and on houses. We saw cars in the canal that apparently floated there. We scurried up the levee to see the breach area and took pictures. We were unable to pass through the checkpoint to get into the New Orleans area. We were trying to possibly get to Mike's Dad's house. We plan to get there this week or next. My feelings of despair deepened, not for myself but for the Metro New Orleans area. It is not the same as watching it on television. You cannot describe it, you have to be here and see it firsthand to fathom the enormity of Katrina's damage. I couldn't even count the number of affected or imagine the dollars for repairs. I try to imagine the art, the photos, the collections and more that are irretrievable. My mind then expands those concepts to the lost jobs, the lost businesses, and the setbacks of unpaid debts. The economic impact is beyond comprehension at this point, but I know it will be long, long lasting.

I now find myself as a stranger in my own town. The Northshore that has sprung back so vigorously is now inundated with relief workers, rescue workers, utility workers, and displaced evacuees. The already booming parish (one of the fastest in the nation) that had infrastructure issues before the storm finds itself exploding to the point of absurdity. I grew up here. It was a small town or cluster of towns (Abita Springs, Mandeville and Covington). It grew with New Orleans transplants that sought refuge from a bustling and hurried city for their after-work life. The highways had just been widened in some parts because of increased population. Now it is the New-New Orleans. The traffic is a parking lot, the stores packed, the lines long and the cost…well the cost is the lifestyle I had so long been accustomed to. I can only hope that it eases as time goes on or who knows…I may seek a new life elsewhere after all. Katrina may have yet another victim who leaves home, never to return.

Sunday (10/2/05)

I have been to the city today. Somehow the tears flowed spontaneously as I further grasped the situation. No, it is not the situation, the collapse or ruin that IS NEW ORLEANS. Can the city ever recover from this bullet in the heart? It is the vitality that existed in her people; the lives ever changed now following the storm, the business failure from lack of income, the government collapse from the collective economic impact that translates into no tax base.

Mike and I started in New Orleans East. My first view is of the many boats on the side of the I-12 and I-610. My

49

mind begins to conceptualize the rising water and blocked exits to safety. As we drive, we see to our left and right, house after house, structure after structure, this one a tree, that one no roof, the next one, fallen wall. Block after block, it is the same. We pass three large car dealerships in the East full to capacity of new inventory, all covered in brown silt, evidence of entire ruin by floodwaters. That alone sent my brain into calculator mode as I ticked off the millions of dollars lost. Our scenic drive began on Chef Mentuer Hwy. We laugh when we see a dead alligator on the side the road, but we didn't laugh again for a while. It becomes apparent that Chef Hwy is the 'high ground.' The side streets into residential areas slope downward. As I see more boats at the end of the streets 'parked' near Chef Hwy, Mike makes me realize that these were escape vessels. We counted thirteen boats on just one street. There were others on street after street. It finally dawns on me that there are no people around. A few stray cars are seen, and maybe a person or two, but that is all. The city is abandoned, desolate, and empty. I can see why! The water line is visible on every structure, the damage to buildings almost inconceivable. I cannot describe it in mere words. Each structure suffered differently, broken glass, total collapse, partial collapse, no collapse, but dirt and debris piled high. The roads that had not been scraped were covered in varying types of settlement; from fine brown silt to mucky, thick and (now) dried, cracked mud. There was 'trashy' debris and 'contents' debris of every sort scattered along the road, around the buildings, on top of things. There were cars upside down. There were cars sideways. In one neighborhood, all the residents had moved cars to the 'neutral ground' (median) to escape any street flooding. Little did they know that it wouldn't matter at all. These cars were under water completely as evidences by their covering with silt. Trees, of course, had all been ripped down as if they were blades of grass being stepped on by the giant, Katrina. Live oaks, centuries old, stood brown and apparently dead in City Park. That was another visual layer to the chaos. The color brown dominated the scenery. There was no green grass, colorful flowers, shrubs, plants…All dead and brown…all withered and brown… all dirty and brown. City Park was dead. On occasion, as we passed, we would stumble on a green patch. We could see the water had not reached that point. But those points were very few. We continued this way through Gentilly, in to the Lakeview area. Here the water line was the highest that we had seen. But the scene was the same or worse. Houses had floated to other yards or streets. A corvette stood hood down, rear side up on a tree. I didn't even recognize the street that we were on when we came to my in-laws house. The beautiful canopy of oaks that lined General Diaz simply didn't exist anymore. A few trees were standing but the shade and greenery was now just a pleasant memory of the beauty of past days. I had seen the pictures of the inside, and could now visualize it without going into the structure now. It saddened me to think of the lovely memories of Christmas, and holidays spent on Ms. Geri's lovely patio with green ferns, wind chimes, and a trickling fountain - all debris and ruin and brown. I stifled another sob as we quietly passed by; neither of us really wanting to comment on anything. At that moment, words would have been hollow in the now empty place in our hearts that existed. We rode silently until we reached the 17th street canal on Veterans (crossing into Metairie and out of Orleans parish). I watched blankly as we left the brown images into life and greenery. I have described it to some as though watching a black-and-white movie as it turns into Technicolor. The difference was so marked that it startled me. The ghost town and twilight zone changed in a blink when we crossed and we could see traffic lights, cars, people, buildings, commerce, and life coming back to Jefferson Parish. Mike even told me of his journey to work each morning going south on the Causeway. Traveling that way you see to the right is Jefferson Parish and to the left is Orleans Parish. In the early morning hours before dawn, the right is twinkling with lights. The left is lonely and dark. I have a sad sinking feeling that New Orleans will never be the same for most residents. I know that for me, it cannot offer me the feeling of belonging and joy I once knew. I have my memories and those I will treasure as my New Orleans.

Katrina – Beacon of Hope

<u>Reconstruction (September – October, 2005)</u>

The statistics are startling Katrina was the third in intensity to hit the United States since 1851, when record-keeping began, according to the National Weather Service. The list is as follows:

Hurricane	Year	Barometric Pressure	Wind speed
		(at landfall)	
Labor Day	1935	26.35/822	160
Camille	1969	26.84/909	190
Katrina	2005	27.11/918	140
Andrew	1992	27.23/922	165

Of the top four, two made landfall in Louisiana. They were Camille and Katrina. Three affected the New Orleans area; they were Camille, Katrina and Andrew. Andrew made landfall in Florida initially but came ashore as a Category 3 Hurricane in south central Louisiana. It turned a bit eastward towards our area and dumped flooding rain throughout. It was more of a rain event for us vs. a wind event like Katrina.

By all accounts, Katrina has impacted not only the state, but also the country. Oil supply was halted which drove gas prices sky high. (The benefit to this was that people in the government realized the value of little ole Luziane). Goods normally transported up river were absent in cities and towns throughout the country. Unemployment in Louisiana for September posted the highest ever at 11.5 percent and 9.6 percent for Mississippi as reported by the US Dept of Labor, Bureau of Labor Statistics. The cost in damages estimated over $250 billion Some other numbers for comparison are:

Description	Katrina**	Andrew (NHC)*
Structures destroyed	140,000	25,000
Cars destroyed	350,000	Unknown
Boats destroyed	60,000	Unknown
Refrigerators/ Washers	> 1 million	unknown
Costs	$ >25 Billion *	$25 Billion

*National Hurricane Center Statistics
** Reported estimates at this time

In these past weeks, life has normalized to a certain level for those of us on the Northshore of Lake Pontchartrain in West St. Tammany Parish. Power is restored to most of this area. The businesses are buzzing with activity but have limited hours because of the lack of employees. There are 'Now Hiring' signs for most businesses. I wondered how this could be when it seemed that there was extreme crowding in stores, streets and restaurants. Although some of the relief has left for the assistance with Hurricane Rita in western Louisiana and now Hurricane Wilma in Florida, there are still plenty of construction, tree, debris, telephone, electric and phone workers that boost the population in the area. In addition, many households have displaced family and/or friends staying with them or in RV's parked in driveways. This means that indeed the population is larger, but are not necessarily people looking for jobs. The shortage of workers has created a wage war among companies McDonald's is offering 8.75/

hour for crew members, while Burger King is wooing labor with a sign-on bonus of $6,000 (paid out over 1 year). Many houses are clear of the trees on their rooftops, but construction and replacement of household items is still in progress. We have decided to try to sell our rental properties. There is a boom in the real estate market making the timing right during this peak. For us, it is the prime opportunity to get the best market value and for those who need housing, it is a home in an area where housing is in short supply and growing shorter each day. There are absolutely no rentals, no RV park spaces, and even no hotels for many miles around.

The insurance adjuster came by and will be allowing us to claim the fence line which was just completed a week before the storm. The fence had at least 44 trees on it. Although our claim isn't critical to our living situation, it feels good that the cost of the improvement to our property will be covered. Many adjusters are still in town as well trying to visit all those who have claims, which amounts to most households. Allstate Insurance has announced that they won't be renewing homeowners' policy as policies come up for renewal. They will make good on the claims, but the losses incurred has hit them hard this quarter I have serious doubts that they have suffered over the long run. All those many years' of premiums for all those households and those of policy holders all over the country and the investment earnings surely amounted to more than the claims for this one event, albeit an extensive and immediate payout. I also know that insurance carriers buy re-insurance with aggregate deductibles to cover themselves (and share risk) that would definitely have been met. If they shared the risk and even if they had losses this quarter to a phenomenal amount, no one has reported the earnings/losses numbers for the past five or even ten years. I find it insulting and demeaning to think that this company should turn its back on those who contributed to their success these many years. It's just another example of the greed that is predominant in insurance companies. It's not really about 'being in good hands' as stated by their marketing, but about being in hands that take your money, but abandon you when they have to live up to their obligations and more importantly when people really need them.

New Orleans is suffering much worse than the congestion problems here. Businesses are slow to return, and people have so much to do, it is overwhelming. Mayor Ray Nagin threw out this 'Casino District' idea as a way to zap life into the city. It received much criticism and rightfully so. No one wants gambling as a way to boost the economy and especially since it will destroy some of the nostalgia and identity that is New Orleans. The culture, architecture, music, food, and colorful history are the identifying features that make the city unique. Most cities throughout the country have some form of the same old thing that casinos offer. It is truly mundane! The casinos are only neon, overrated imitations of what is truly entertaining. Entertainment, wonder and the unique are what tourists want to embrace in order to taste a different style and flavor that is new to them. Besides, many people are missing the really significant feature of New Orleans, the River! The river is what made New Orleans valuable to the nation throughout history.

The river and the port are the backbone of the city and should be the focus as the city finds the basis upon which to build. The river is an everlasting and solid natural resource that is the heart and soul of New Orleans and has been from the earliest days of New Orleans when the majestic Mississippi River was used for travel, transport, sustenance, and recreation. It is also fundamentally important to the safety and wellbeing of our country. The river is the artery of the United States giving life and growth to the very heart of our country. Tourism can never provide that kind of security and permanence. In lean times, tourism wanes. This is being horribly and really exemplified by Katrina's toll. Too much emphasis has been placed on tourist dollars. Had enhancements to the port been equally financed, New Orleans would not be suffering as badly today because already the port is operational and, in fact, much more needed by the rest of the country. Instead, many are making an issue over the Saints and whether Tom Benson is moving them to San Antonio permanently or not. They see this as a loss to the economy and it is. I won't cry if the Saints leave. There will be time to grow and develop a new and better city and in the future, create incentives to attract teams on the city's terms instead of the other way around. This controversy is just an example of the ugliness brought out by Katrina's devastation. Professional sports have lost the sense of the game as enjoyment for players and fans as their primary mission, and has become only greed-driven businesses. If you look at high school football, it really drives the point home. These players work and drill all year for the sake of the one winning game. The fans come out and cheer the home team and love it. The Friday night stadium has an aura, and the school spirit reigns. And all that is gained, with the cost of admission, is maybe some new equipment for next year. I would much prefer if the Saints left New Orleans and we could move on.

Reconstruction continues and as it does, I see more fully the time that is needed to bring this area back to pre-Katrina days. The mayor of New Orleans makes bold claims of more population than pre-Katrina in five years. Mike and I both scoffed at this when we heard it. I cannot see that in five years. If the levees are secured to Category 5 storm levels, it might happen within 7 years. If they aren't, it will be at least 10 years. It will have to be enough time for young people to grow old enough to invest in New Orleans and have little memory of this unimaginable event.

Yet, no matter the number of beats of the clock that pass, Katrina is still a moment in time carved in my soul. We didn't suffer greatly, but I sampled enough to be scarred from the encounter. I witnessed complete destruction and despair that changed my world and my reality. It is for me a moment when I learned to value life more dearly. It is a turning point when I began to meditate on the truths of my life and family and career. It is when I could reach out to others and it meant something. It was a feeling a being lost and now found safe and secure. It was an upheaval of the neat package of society where we all feel safe, comfortable, and empowered as sovereign. It was a face-to-face encounter with the earth's natural destructive power that tossed the fruits of our years of toil like it was blades of grass under the shoe of a giant. Katrina is a gleaming, glowing beacon in my memory that continues to signal me to be prepared, to show love, to value time, pray always, and respect all of Gods creation, always.

View of Downs Avenue from our driveway facing south.

View of Downs Ave from our driveway facing north after clearing to the corner (see telephone box at intersection)

Views (above & below) from corner of Downs & Lowe Davis Road
looking down Lowe Davis These are the trees already cut by us. We
are near the truck you see in the distance still working.

Corner of Downs Ave & Lowe Davis Road facing towards the continuation of Downs

Signs posted in neighborhoods all over the Northshore area.

Scariano home condition after Katrina (view of front of home)

Scariano home with trees removed (view of right side of home as you face the house)

Tree on my car

09.15.2005

View of Lowe Davis Road two weeks after the storm after the road is cleared Count the number of tree stubs in just this area!

Entire metal roof peeled off on building in Covington It lay on the ground in crumbles.

Picture of outside of my in-laws home; Edgar & Geri

Inside of my Edgar & Geri's home Ceiling tile is all gone, furniture floated all around and fan blades are drooping from 3 weeks of around 10 ft of water.

Another view of Edgar & Geri's See water line at top of wall.

View of home in New Orleans See water line on home Also note the bush is brown from standing water but top is green that could still obtain sunlight The dull brown on street is sediment.

Note cars parked in median to avoid any anticipated street-flooding They are covered in residue from being covered completely with water.

Boats left behind by people as they reached the high ground of the highway There were 13 boats at this one intersection.

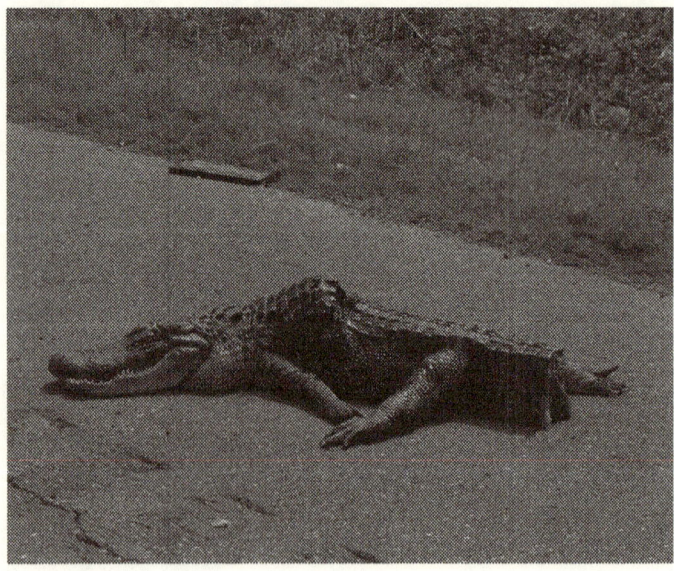

Poor gator didn't make it through the storm… someone cut the tail for the meat.